That's not my...
colouring book
Dinosaurs

This book belongs to...

_____

That's not my big dinosaur.

That's my
—— dinosaur.

That's not my
spiky dinosaur.

That's my
———— dinosaur.

That's not my
lumpy dinosaur.

That's my
dinosaur.
—— —— ——

That's not my long dinosaur.

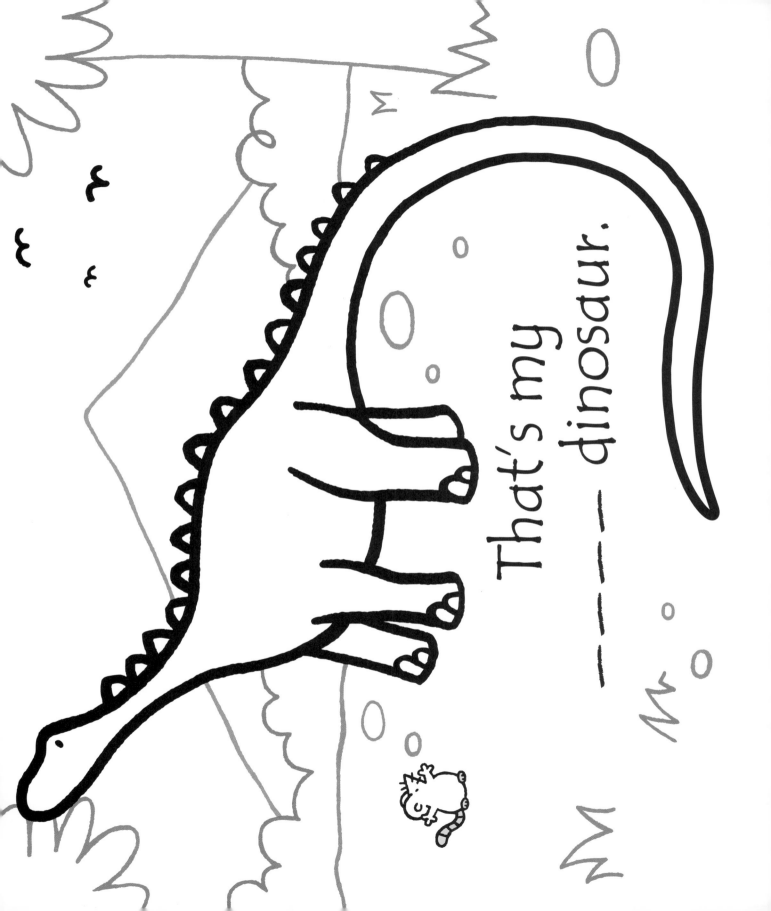

That's my
—————— dinosaur.

That's not my swimming
dinosaur.

That's my _____
dinosaur.

That's not my
noisy dinosaur.

That's my
_____ dinosaur.

That's not my spotty dinosaur.

That's my ———— dinosaur.

That's not my bumpy dinosaur.

That's my
—— —— dinosaur.

That's not my
tall dinosaur.

That's my
_ _ _ _ _ dinosaur.

That's not my
scaly dinosaur.

That's my
———— dinosaur.

That's not my
large dinosaur.

That's my
——— dinosaur.

That's not my
fat dinosaur.

That's my
—— dinosaur.

That's not my
angry dinosaur.

That's my
_ _ _ _ _ _ _ dinosaur.

Can you finish these dinosaurs?

Draw teeth in the mouth.

Draw spots on the body.

Draw three horns
on the head.

Draw spikes
on its back.

Colour the dinosaurs and learn their names.

Plesiosaur

Brachiosaurus

Allosaurus

Parasaurolophus

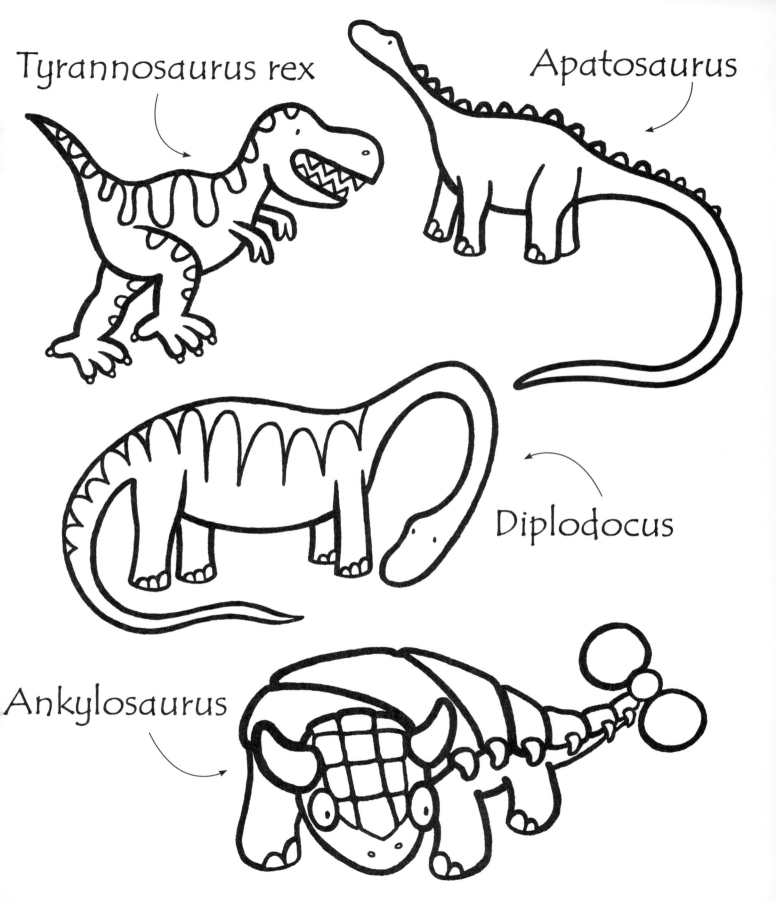

Tyrannosaurus rex

Apatosaurus

Diplodocus

Ankylosaurus

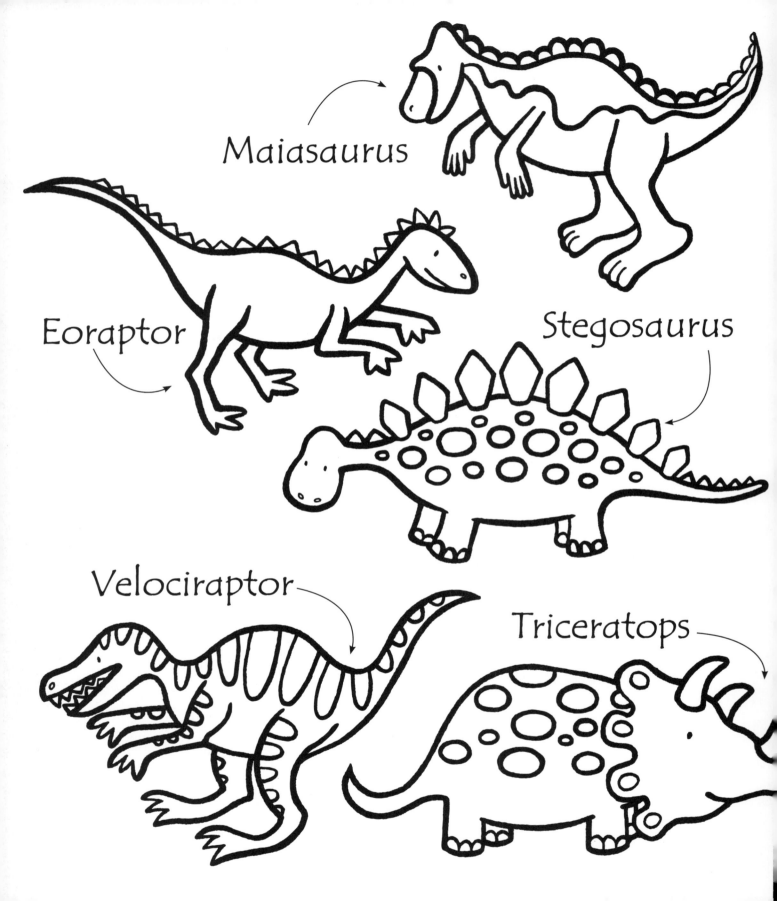

Maiasaurus

Eoraptor

Stegosaurus

Velociraptor

Triceratops